GRIMSBY
IN OLD PHOTOGRAPHS

WELLOWGATE, c. 1908. The small boy standing outside Joseph Dixon's fruit shop is F. Grange, aged nine, who grew up to take over the Mayfield Dairies, also in Wellowgate.

GRIMSBY
IN OLD PHOTOGRAPHS

COLLECTED BY
JANET TIERNEY

ALAN SUTTON

Alan Sutton Publishing Limited
Phoenix Mill · Far Thrupp · Stroud · Gloucestershire

First published 1990

British Library Cataloguing in Publication Data

Grimsby in old photographs.
1. Humberside. Grimsby, history
I. Tierney, Janet
942.834

ISBN 0-86299-647-3

Front cover illustration:
THE RIVERHEAD C. 1900, a hive of commercial activity. The *Quenast* was a regular visitor to
the port.

Typeset in 9/10 Korinna.
Typesetting and origination by
Alan Sutton Publishing Limited.
Printed in Great Britain
by Dotesios Printers Limited.

CONTENTS

GRIMSBY TOWN STATION in the 1860s, when it served the Great Northern and the Manchester, Sheffield and Lincolnshire Railways. Access to the platforms was fairly rudimentary; there was no footbridge at this date, and passengers had to cross the line by means of the board walk in the foreground.

INTRODUCTION

Historians today are making increasing use of photographs as primary archives, instead of purely illustrative material to complement documentary research. Photographs breathe life into the past by clarifying so much that can only be inferred – often erroneously – from a written source that assumes knowledge of the writer's subject, and by challenging our own culturally- biased assumptions about what the past was really like. It does, of course, have to be remembered that with portraits of people and premises taken by professional photographers, part of the object of the exercise was to show the subject in its best possible light, so that pictures of shop-fronts – like that of Edward Hotson's game dealer's shop in this collection – or of tradesmens' groups, might not be a completely accurate representation of how the shop really looked every other day of the week, or of how brewers or carpenters normally dressed for work. Like any other document, photographs can present an idealized picture of the real world if not handled with due circumspection.

The first professional photographer recorded as operating in Grimsby was one William Gothard, who had a studio in Victoria Street South. Although he appears to have gone out of business by the end of the 1860s, others came to take his place, and Grimsby has been most fortunate in being served by a large number of professional photographers, such as William Audas, the Lowthian Brothers and Walter Marsden in the nineteenth century, and Stanley Warren and Sid and Roland Burton in the twentieth, to mention just a few. Together with many amateurs, unfortunately by and large anonymous, their pictures have left a fascinating record of the town over nearly 140 years.

The photographs in this book have been selected to give a broad picture of the townscape and the people of Grimsby over the century between 1860 and 1960. The earliest surviving photographs in fact date from the late 1850s and 1860s, and show a townscape that is basically familiar (or at least readily identifiable) at the centre, but which becomes increasingly less so within a very short distance of it. It comes perhaps as something of a surprise to discover that parts of Grimsby – such as Flottergate or Wellowgate – which today are very much a part of the built-up area, presented a distinctly rural face to the camera as comparatively recently as 1870. The photographs also remind us that Grimsby was an important market town for this north-eastern corner of Lindsey, sufficiently important for a Corn Exchange and Butter Market to be built in the Old Market Place in 1858. Because of the importance of the docks to the town throughout the period covered by this book, Grimsby's role in servicing a large and rich agricultural hinterland often assumes a background role.

That Grimsby was a major cultural centre in north Lincolnshire in the late nineteenth and early twentieth centuries can also be seen here, with several capacious theatres and a plethora of cinemas, and dance and music halls, not to mention a flourishing private zoo. Pictures of the wealth of churches and chapels of different denominations indicate a diverse and thriving religious life also. The photographs of charity parades and galas, the portraits of members of the many sporting and social clubs in the town, and candid shots of Grimbarians simply enjoying themselves in a wide variety of ways all indicate the gradual evolution of the rich and distinct social fabric of a town full of life and vigour.

The Grimsby of the nineteenth-century photographers was essentially the creation of the railway companies. With a population at the 1801 census of 1524, and little more than a large village at the end of the eighteenth century, the borough was rescued from its state of near-terminal decay by the building of what came to be known as 'the Old Dock', by the Grimsby Haven Company. Until that time it had little more to recommend it, other than its borough status, than most of the other little havens on the Humber. The existence of the dock (which was very much in the doldrums because of the poor inland communications) and Grimsby's geographically advantageous position at the mouth of the Humber, suggested that rather more could be made of the port, and there were various proposals, none of which came to anything until the Great Grimsby and Sheffield Junction Railway Company, under the chairmanship of Lord Worsley, came into being. The line was duly opened in 1848 (after the original company had been taken over by the Manchester, Sheffield and Lincolnshire Railway) and the nascent port duly flourished. Another speculative venture was also set in hand, under the aegis of the railway company – the building of what was ultimately called the Royal Dock.

No photographs appear to have survived which show either the construction of the Royal Dock (one has to rely on J.W. Carmichael's well-known painting for that) or which document Queen Victoria's visit to the town in 1854. From the 1860s, however, photographs of the dockscape and dock activity proliferate. The various aspects of the port's trade are all very well represented: the grain barges and Humber keels at the Riverhead, the graceful Norwegian ice barques, the colliers and ore carriers and, of course, the cod smacks, herring drifters and trawlers which have come to epitomize Grimsby. Grimsby's excellent railway communications with most of Britain, and particularly the capital, together with its readiness to accommodate the fishing vessels, made it especially attractive to the smacks from the south and west coast migrating up to the Dogger Bank and North Sea in search of fresh fishing grounds and better access to potential markets. The movement began in the 1850s and gathered increasing momentum throughout the century, and these vessels, together with the steam trawlers which replaced them, are represented in this collection of photographs.

Another aspect of Grimsby's port activities captured by the camera were the emigrants who flooded into the port throughout the century *en route* to Liverpool and the United States. Some (probably the majority) were fleeing from the various persecutions of religious and other minorities in Europe throughout the century; others were economic migrants in search of opportunity; others were political refugees. Sid Gold (the oldest surviving participant of the 1905 Russian Revolution), who arrived in Grimsby on a fishing boat, was fleeing from the consequences of blowing up the tsar's ministers. Many of the emigrants never got as far even as Liverpool, settling in Grimsby and helping to give the town its refreshingly cosmopolitan flavour.

All the photographs in this book belong to the Grimsby Museum Service at the Welholme Galleries. Many formed part of the collections of the late W.E.R. ('Bill') Hallgarth, schoolmaster, sportsman and local historian, an avid collector of photographs not only of Grimsby but the entire county of Lincolnshire. The remainder have either been donated to the museum or copied from originals loaned for that purpose by local people.

The Changing Face of Grimsby

HIGH STREET, as this part of the Old Market Place was called at this time, taken in the 1870s. The arch next to Goodwin's Eating House (later Turner's, the drapers) was a right-of-way leading into the Bull Ring. William Marshall, the proprietor of the Saddlery, is standing on the right.

THE OLD MARKET PLACE on a spring day in 1905, from the station approach.

OLD MARKET PLACE, C. 1900, looking across to Bull Ring Lane which, as the name suggests, led into the Bull Ring. All this side of the street disappeared in the remodelling of Top Town in the 1960s.

TWO VIEWS OF THE MARKET PLACE, taken at the Friday Market in the summer of 1937.

THE OLD MARKET PLACE, photographed about 1930. The Market Place was enlarged in the middle of the nineteenth century, when the Corporation borrowed £5,000 and purchased and demolished a large range of old buildings on the site of what was Butcher Lane. The Corn Exchange and Market Hall were erected in part of this newly-created space in 1856 at a cost of £3,500.

VICTORIA STREET SOUTH C. 1860. Until Queen Victoria's visit to Grimsby in 1854, the street was known as Loft Street, named by the Corporation in 1809 after Major General John Henry Loft, briefly MP for Grimsby at this time.

VICTORIA STREET, pictured in the early 1860s. While pavements were laid there in 1855, the road itself still appears to be in a natural state, with ruts and puddles abounding. The woman in the centre of the photograph, poised to cross the road, has hitched her crinoline up out of harm's way.

VICTORIA STREET in 1881, looking down the street towards the Riverhead. The garden, with its fine, mature elm trees, marks the site of the present Midland Bank, while beyond, the fascia of the new Queen's Head public house can be seen, now replaced by the modern Woolworth's building.

THE GEORGIAN TOWN HALL, which stood in the Old Market Place, replacing the original medieval building which was pulled down in 1780. Councillors shared the building with the town gaol and courthouse, and this unsatisfactory arrangement continued up to 1863, when the present Town Hall was opened. The Georgian building lingered on as a school until 1868, when it went the way of its medieval predecessor. This picture was taken in 1860, by William Skelton.

ST JAMES' CHURCH, taken from the Deansgate Bridge in the 1880s.

SILVER STREET C. 1873, from the Victoria Street end, looking towards the river with Marshall's steam flour mill looming hazily in the distance. The Mason's Arms, managed at this date by one Charles Henry Plumpton (who doubled up his beer retailing with poultry and pigeon dealing), is in the centre of the picture and the Silver Street Chapel is at the extreme end of the street.

RUS IN URBE? The pocked and rutted road with no pavement, the haystack, and the traditional thatched mud and stud cottage are all suggestive of a rural setting, but the photograph was in fact taken in Wellowgate at the end of the 1860s or early 1870s judging by the women's dress. The tower bell-turret of the mock-Tudor Corn Exchange can be seen at the side of the haystack.

THE TOWN HALL in 1904, a 'very complete pile of buildings' containing 'all the various apartments required for the transaction of the public business of a corporate town . . .' The building, designed in the Italianate style so popular in the mid-nineteenth century, was opened with a suitably magnificent banquet given by the Mayor, Henry Bennett, on 15 October 1863.

THE COUNCIL CHAMBER OF THE PRESENT TOWN HALL, shortly after its opening in 1863. The magnificent furniture made for the new buildings is still in use.

GRIMSBY HAD A NUMBER OF MILLS in the mid-nineteenth century, by no means all of them for processing grain. This is Norfolk's bone mill in East Marsh Street, near the site of the present-day ASDA supermarket. The mill was used for crushing bone and seeds, linseed oil being extracted from the latter and cattle cake produced from the residue. The photograph was taken c. 1865.

HOLLINGWORTH'S POST-MILL at Cartergate in the 1860s.

MISS MILNER'S SCHOOL IN MAUDE STREET, *c.* 1860. This was what was known as a Dame School: an elementary school run, as the name suggests, by a woman who would charge her pupils 3d. or 4d. a week for lessons. The education received was very variable, depending on the competence or otherwise of the 'dame'. At best, they could provide a good basic grounding in the 'three Rs'; at worst, they were little more than glorified child-minding centres. Dame schools like Miss Milner's were very common until local authority-run board schools began to be set up under the 1870 Education Act.

FLOTTERGATE CHAPEL, on the corner of Maude Street, 'an edifice' according to *Kelly's Directory*, 'of red brick with stone dressings'. It could seat a congregation of 1,050, making it one of the largest of Grimsby's Nonconformist chapels. The photograph was taken *c.*1910 by Grimsby photographer J.S. Bullen of Freeman Street.

THE RED-BRICK BAPTIST TABERNACLE in Victoria Street, near to the present Hope & Anchor pub, built in 1876 by John Brown in a style described rather vaguely as 'Romanesque'. The photograph was probably taken towards the end of the nineteenth century.

THE BOOKING HALL AND FORECOURT, Grimsby Town station, pictured in the 1890s.

GRIMSBY TOWN STATION in the summer of 1902. The black smudge on the fretwork canopy is not some photographic defect, but was rather the result of the smoke from the steam engine striking it as it passed underneath.

CHANTRY LANE, looking from the Bull Ring, taken in the late 1920s.

LOOKING TOWARDS WHAT HAS NOW BECOME ALEXANDRA ROAD FROM FLOTTERGATE, with Flottergate House on the right in front of the fine chimney of Marshall's flour mill. The photograph was taken during the 1870s.

THE ELEGANT GAS-HOLDER at the Sheepfold Street gasworks. The original gasworks were established in 1837 in Loft Street (later renamed Victoria Street) by one Richard Holme. They were transferred by a group of shareholders to Holme Street in 1851, and to Sheepfold Street later in the century.

DOUGHTY ROAD SUBWAY in the 1950s, dominated by the cooling towers of the Moss Road power station. The Borough's electricity supply was originally the responsibility of Grimsby Corporation, a role which was shed following the nationalization of the electricity industry and the creation of the Central Electricity Generating Board.

TRAMWAY REPAIRS IN FREEMAN STREET, c. 1910. The tramways system in Grimsby was originally run by the Provincial Tramways Company, but this part of their undertaking was bought out, after going to arbitration, by Grimsby Corporation in December 1924.

LOOKING TOWARDS HAINTON SQUARE from the corner of Garibaldi Street in the 1920s.

THE NEW MARKET STREET FOOTBRIDGE in 1871, shortly after it opened. The bridge linked the Central Market with Freeman Street, and the new market there which opened in 1873. The footbridge was built by Head, Wrightson & Co. of Stockton-on-Tees, the same firm responsible for the original 1873 swing-bridge across the Alexandra Dock.

THE NEW MARKET STREET FOOTBRIDGE in 1872, with the coal sidings below.

THE OPEN-AIR MARKET, created in 1873 on the freemen's land in Freeman Street to serve what had become the most densely-populated part of town. The spire to the right of the photograph, taken c. 1905, belonged to St Andrew's church. The photographer has obviously decided that it did not stand out sufficiently well, and has subtly enhanced his work with a pencil!

FREEMAN STREET MARKET, taken in the summer of 1914.

SUMMER IN FREEMAN STREET in the 1890s. The young lady bowling down the road on her safety bicycle appears to be wearing a pair of bloomers, an example of late Victorian rational dress which, in a small provincial town like Grimsby, would even by this date have been considered fairly daring.

FREEMAN STREET in the 1930s, looking towards Riby Square. The impressive building in the centre of the photograph is Waby's outfitters, at No. 101 Cleethorpe Road.

THE PRINCE OF WALES THEATRE, on the right, shortly after it opened in 1886. The simple porch at the main entrance was eventually replaced by a far more elaborate canopy running right across the front of the building.

THE CORPORATION HOTEL in Freeman Street in the 1860s. The gap in the building line was later filled, in 1869, by the Zion Baptist Chapel.

REDHILL, in the early 1920s. The street, built in the 1830s, ran from one side of the Flottergate Primitive Methodist Church down to Cartergate, where its continuation was the present-day Lord Street. The street is supposed to have acquired its name from the reputed political convictions of the residents, the 'Reds' of the 1830s being the Whigs who became known as 'Liberals' as the century progressed.

PLEASANT CONVERSATION AT THE CORNER OF ROBINSON STREET AND PASTURE STREET c. 1920. Just visible in the background, dwarfing the houses, is the Consolidated Steam Fishing & Ice Company's ice factory.

CENTRAL MARKET, C. 1875, with the triangular pediment of the Theatre Royal and Marshall's mill chimney on Victoria Street visible in the background. The clock tower was presented to the Borough in 1870 by coal merchant Edward Bannister, during his mayoral year. It was demolished in 1959, and the clock was removed to Cadwell Park.

CLEETHORPE ROAD AND THE DOCK CROSSING, taken at the end of the nineteenth century. On the right is the Royal Hotel or, to give it its full title, The Royal Dock Hotel, described as 'a large, handsome and commodious building, in the Italian style of architecture, fitted with all modern requirements'. The hotel was built 1864/5 by John Brown of Pasture Street, and demolished just over a century later in 1966.

CLEETHORPE ROAD in the mid-1920s, looking towards Riby Square.

THE PRIMITIVE METHODIST CHAPEL on Cleethorpe Road built in 1864, and photographed here *c.* 1870. The site was later used in the 1930s for the Premier Cinema, and its successor, the Plaza.

THE GRIMSBY–LOUTH 'MOTOR' TRAIN, stopped at Weelsby Halt on Weelsby Road in the 1920s.

WEELSBY ROAD, GRIMSBY.

WEELSBY ROAD in the 1920s, curiously devoid of traffic by late twentieth-century standards.

NUN'S CORNER, taken c. 1900, looking down Scartho Road. Grimsby is signposted to the right, Brigg to the left.

NUN'S FARM, still in agricultural use at the time that this photograph was taken, c. 1905, by William Marshall. The farmhouse was built on the site of the Augustinian nunnery of St Leonard, founded some time before 1184 and dissolved in 1539. The farmhouse itself was demolished in 1935, and the site is now occupied by the College of Technology.

THE ABBEY, one-time home of the influential Wintringham family. It was built on the site of the medieval Wellow Abbey, another victim of Henry VIII.

THE STABLES at the Willows on Bargate, the home of William Grange.

CLARENCE TERRACE IN ABBEY ROAD, often known as Spectacle Row on account of its unusual (in Grimsby, at least) circular dormer windows. This elegant terrace of sixteen houses was built in 1865. The photograph below shows the completed buildings.

THE FOUNDATION STONE for the new Grimsby & District Hospital, built to replace earlier premises in Cleethorpe Road, was laid on a site in the West Marsh, now South Parade, by the Countess of Yarborough on 17 July 1876. Just under a year later, the plain gothic building was opened by the countess. Further wings and facilities were added, and the resultant accretions were officially opened by the 4th Earl of Yarborough in 1933. The photograph shows the completed hospital in the 1930s.

Bottom, right:

THE OLD CEMETERY was built on poorly-drained land – hence the drainage windmill – and rapidly became overcrowded, a new cemetery having to be opened off Scartho Road in 1889. The old cemetery was eventually abandoned, the gravestones removed, and the area transformed into the Ainslie Street recreation ground of today.

THE ENTRANCE TO THE OLD BOROUGH CEMETERY at what was the end of Garden Street, taken in the 1860s. The cemetery had been formed in 1855, after the passing of the 1853 Burial Act permitted local authorities to administer their own cemeteries. It contained two mortuary chapels, the one being somewhat fancifully described 'Early Decorated' and the other 'Early English' style.

A PETROL-DRIVEN OMNIBUS, owned by the Provincial Tramways Company, driving through the great cast-iron gates at the Ainslie Street entrance to People's Park, c. 1910.

FAIRFIELD AVENUE, SCARTHO, taken in the early 1950s, and as yet unadopted. The photograph was taken by P. Jackson of Pinfold Lane.

SECTION TWO

The Port of Grimsby

SOUTH DOCK STREET in the 1890s, which ran from Victoria Street alongside the Riverhead. In the distance can be seen the ribs of a vessel under construction in one of the yards in the Old Dock – Alexandra Dock area.

ICE BARQUES IN THE ROYAL DOCK, C. 1890. Many of the smacks which came to Grimsby in the 1850s were 'well-vessels'. The catch was kept alive and, after landing at Grimsby, was stored in floating wooden 'cod chests' in the fish docks. Pollution, congestion, and changing technology meant that this system was superseded by the use of ice, at first pond ice, used in a rudimentary cold store, and increasingly after 1857, Norwegian ice imported via the port of Breveg in these elegant vessels, and then used at sea. Despite the building of ice factories at Grimsby, the Norwegian trade continued up to and after the First World War.

MR SMITH, the dock flag-man, pictured here c. 1890.

A RARE STUDIO PORTRAIT OF A SAILING FISHER-MAN, Henry Freshney, taken c. 1870. Freshney was a cod-man at the time this portrait was taken, ten years or so before steam was introduced to Grimsby, and would have worked one of the powerful ketch-rigged North Sea 'cod-bangers'.

A RATHER UNUSUAL PERSPECTIVE OF THE DOCKS, taken from the Cleethorpe side, c. 1890. The forest of masts and general absence of funnels indicate the relatively early date of this photograph; the first steam trawlers made their appearance at Grimsby in 1883.

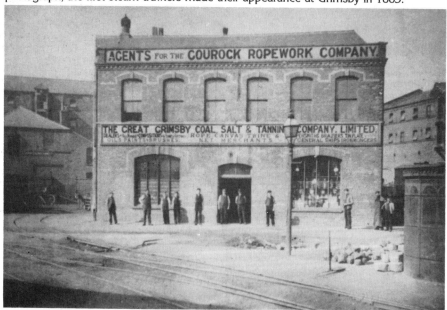

THE ORIGINAL HEADQUARTERS OF THE GREAT GRIMSBY COAL SALT AND TANNING COMPANY from 1873 to 1895. This photograph was taken c. 1880.

THE PRODUCTION OF DRIED SALT COD, and its export, had been an important industry in Grimsby since the Middle Ages. Here, the dried fish are being loaded into rail wagons on the fish docks, c. 1890.

STEAM TRAWLERS at Campbell's Jetty in the 1930s.

PACKING FISH FILLETS on Grimsby Docks. The boy in the foreground is Walter Sparling.

THE PONTOON AT GRIMSBY in the 1890s. The man in the left foreground of the photograph, half turning his head towards the camera, is wearing a seal-skin cap, apparently a favourite type of headgear among the smack skippers. Trawler skippers favoured bowlers on shore.

COD STACKED NEATLY ON THE DOCK SIDE, being eyed speculatively by the two bowler-hatted fish merchants. The picture probably dates from the mid-1920s.

TRAWLERMEN AT WORK ON THE NETS of the Grimsby steam trawler *Orpheus*, c. 1936.

THE HERRING SLIP AT GRIMSBY in the tidal basin of the Royal Dock, photographed during the lean years of the 1930s – hence the fairly low level of activity, by nineteenth-century standards at least. The herring fishing was essentially seasonal, the migrating shoals of the increasingly elusive 'silver darlings' being pursued by vessels from Scotland to Great Yarmouth. The vessels shown here are all steam drifters from Lowestoft.

SCOTS 'HERRING LASSIES' on the herring slip at the turn of the century. The women followed the herring boats from the north of Scotland, working their way through all the east coast ports down to Yarmouth and Lowestoft. It was a desperately tough occupation; they worked outside in all weathers in groups of three, gutting and packing the herrings in salt, which must have caused havoc to chapped or cut hands.

NEW. FISH DOCKS

GRIMSBY'S THIRD AND LAST FISH DOCK was opened in 1934. Costing in the region of £1,650,000, it added 35 acres of water to the total dock area, effectively doubling the capacity, to accommodate the 500 or so vessels operating from the port. This photograph was taken by Stanley Warren shortly after the new dock was opened.

WORK IN PROGRESS ON THE LOCK ENTRANCE to the new No. 3 Fish Dock, taken in September 1933.

THE ENTRANCE to the 45 ft lock nearing completion. The photograph was taken on 8 January 1934 by Sid Burton.

THE CONSTRUCTION OF THE NEW FISH DOCK in the early 1930s necessitated a crossing of the main Grimsby–Cleethorpes railway line. A level crossing was clearly out of the question – the dock crossing further down on Cleethorpe Road was often quoted as the world's busiest railway crossing, and a bridge had to be built at Humber Street. This photograph, taken in May 1932, shows the ramp under construction.

THE QUEEN MARY HOSTEL, run by the Royal National Mission to Deep Sea Fishermen at Riby Square–Orwell Street, in 1930.

THE STEAM TRAWLER *ARSENAL*, one in a line of trawlers owned by Consolidated Fisheries Ltd named after football clubs. She was built by Cook, Welton & Gemmell Ltd of Beverley, and her engines were produced by C.D. Holmes & Co. of Hull.

THE END OF THE *ARSENAL*, lying dismembered in the breaker's yard at Fleetwood in 1976. Its undignified demise is grimly symbolic of the crumbling of the Grimsby fishing industry as a whole in the face of the 'cod wars', over-fishing in the North Sea, and what many in the industry perceived as its betrayal by the government in the negotiations over the EEC Common Fisheries Policy.

THE DOCKS, C. 1900.

NAVVIES EXCAVATING THE UNION DOCK in the 1870s. The Union Dock was the channel which connected the original Grimsby Haven Company's 1801 Dock and the new Alexandra Dock with the 1852 Royal Dock.

CLINKER-BUILT HUMBER SLOOPS at the Riverhead, c. 1875.

BLOW'S LANDING STAGE and the *Basalt* being unloaded, 1920s.

A DECEPTIVELY TRANQUIL VIEW of the Riverhead at the end of the nineteenth century. The photographs on the preceding page, showing the Riverhead seething with shipping and port activity, are far more typical.

SUBMARINES AT GRIMSBY

GRIMSBY ENJOYED FREQUENT VISITATIONS FROM THE ROYAL NAVY, and was a submarine base during the First World War. These submarines and warship at the port were photographed slightly earlier, in 1908.

THE NEW CORPORATION ROAD LIFTING BRIDGE across the Alexandra Dock, gaily bedecked to welcome 'Our Empire's Ambassador', Edward, Prince of Wales. The bridge, built to replace the exceedingly troublesome 1873 swing-bridge, was designed by the Glasgow firm of Sir William Arrol & Co., whose other works included the Forth Railway Bridge. In civil engineering terms it is of considerable interest as an early example of a rolling bascule construction.

GREEN'S DEAL YARD on the Alexandra Dock, taken in the 1950s. Arther Calder stands second on the left in the group, the others unfortunately have not so far been identified. Grimsby had a long-standing trade in timber with Scandinavia and the Baltic.

SACKS OF MALT for export brought by rail from the Maltings at Newark, being loaded on board ship in the Royal Dock. The photograph was taken by Grimsby professional photographer Roland Burton in the early 1950s.

TIMBER BEING UNLOADED IN THE ROYAL DOCK, 1958. The photograph was taken by Roland Burton of Abbey Road, Grimsby.

FROM THE MIDDLE OF THE NINETEENTH CENTURY, Grimsby became the port of entry for the swelling tide of human misery thrown up by the shameful pogroms, the persecution of Russian Jews instigated by Tsar Alexander II. Many stayed in Grimsby, but the majority travelled by rail to Liverpool and thence to the United States. The Jewish refugees were joined by other migrants from Eastern and Central Europe, notably Moravian Christians, and Mormons. The problems caused by the volume of emigrants led to the conversion of the Royal Dock station c. 1870 to form the Emigrants' Home, which provided temporary dormitory accommodation for about 300 people.

EMIGRANTS ON BOARD SHIP, C. 1900.

Grimsby at Work

FOUNDRY-MEN AT HARPER PHILLIPS' ALBION FOUNDRY sand-casting a trawler propeller in 1933.

THE *GRIMSBY DAILY TELEGRAPH* (or the *Eastern Daily Telegraph* as it was originally known) was founded by Sir George Doughty in 1897. It had a distinctly chequered career in its early stages, but received a much-needed boost with the enormous interest aroused by the Boer War, and, most particularly, by the 1901 dock lock-out.

PACKING COPIES OF THE *GRIMSBY DAILY TELEGRAPH* for despatch in the 1930s.

TWO VIEWS OF THE *TELEGRAPH* WORKS at No. 80 Cleethorpe Road, c. 1910. At this time the newspaper was set by hand, printed on flat-bed machines at a rate of about 500 four-page papers per hour, and then folded by hand.

'BY THE AID OF INSTANTANEOUS PHOTOGRAPHY W. Garthwaite is now producing SPLENDID Portraits of Babies and Young Children. See specimens in the window, ALL of which are produced by W.G.'. William Garthwaite appears to have had mixed fortunes in his career as a commercial photographer, establishing himself in 1877 at No. 187 Cleethorpe Road (seen here), before moving studios several times, interspersed with a short period when he apparently diversified into ice-cream manufacture. He was, as his shop window suggests, a very competent portraitist. Unfortunately, examples of some of his other advertised photographic specialities, such as picnic parties, animals and ships in motion, do not appear to have survived.

Bottom, right:
LAWSON AND STOCKDALE'S PREMISES in Victoria Street, in the 1920s. An interesting commentary on changing customs is provided by the window marked 'Mechanics' Clothing'. Right up to the immediate post-war period, protective work-clothes were sold in the clothiers along with tailor-made costumes and off-the-peg suits. The modern trend, however, is for this type of clothing to be provided by the employer and purchased direct from industrial clothing wholesalers.

THE GREAT GRIMSBY CO-OPERATIVE SOCIETY'S CENTRAL STORE on the corner of Freeman Street and Garibaldi Street, taken c. 1930. The market is to the left of the photograph.

FACTORY GIRLS at Peter Dixon's West Marsh paper mills at Little Coates, in the 1920s.

HARRIS ROSENBURG'S TAILOR'S WORKSHOP at No. 102 Freeman Street, with the clothing order for the Borough Police Force.

HERBERT ROLLETT WAS A FARMER'S SON, born just outside Gainsborough in 1872. Apprenticed to a grocer, he eventually moved to Grimsby, where he opened his own shop, shown here c. 1905, at No. 72 Victoria Street. He began painting at the age of thirty, and shot to fame in 1924, when he had a painting accepted at the Royal Academy. In 1927, he was made an Associate of the Royal Society of British Artists, and a full member the following year. Herbert Rollett died in 1934.

THE PASTURE STREET DAIRY at No. 19 Pasture Street, with Conway's bottling factory and drays, c. 1938.

THIS DELIGHTFUL PICTURE of Charles Shephard's wonderfully congested Freeman Street window, festooned with brushes and Edwardian domestic paraphernalia, must have been taken in 1910 if we believe that the owner repainted his shop-front every year. In his trade directory entry for 1906, Charles and Son describe themselves modestly as 'brush manufacturers and small-ware dealers', which entirely fails to convey the quite enormous range of their stock-in-trade.

Bottom, left:
MR BROCKLESBY DRIVING HIS MILK CART at the back of Humberstone Road in the early 1930s. Julian and Spilsby Dairies, owned by the Curd Brothers (Harold and William) in Julian Street, was one of a large number of small dairies operating in Grimsby in the 1920s and '30s. Milk bought from these dairymen was drawn by the householder direct from the churn, using a tinned iron measure.

A TYPICAL GRIMSBY CORNER SHOP in the late 1940s: Wilke's tobacconists and confectioners, at No. 172 Victoria Street.

AN IMPRESSIVE DISPLAY OF CARCASSES at Edward Hotson's shop at No. 285 Cleethorpe Road, taken c. 1892. The equally impressive sign and cartouche were by painter and decorator Joseph Mundey of Grant Street.

Bottom, left:
JAMES TIERNEY (extreme right) with staff outside his tobacconist's shop at No. 42 Cleethorpe Road, under the sign of the Green Lamp, c. 1925. By the 1920s, when this photograph was taken, Tierney had six shops in Grimsby and one in Cleethorpes and, unusually for that period, a bonded warehouse through which he imported his own tobacco to make his cigars and tobacco blends.

JOHN WARD'S BUTCHER'S SHOP at No. 26 Chantry Lane, taken c. 1910. The open shop-front, with carcasses dangling from hooks in the grill above, is typical of its period.

CHARLES WATMOUGH AND SON originally ran a grocery and ship's stores business from these premises at No. 21 Cleethorpe Road, at the corner of Flower Square. Their Neptune Steam Biscuit Factory at Flower Square was originally used for the manufacture of ship's biscuits, but later diversified into more gastronomically exciting products and moved the expanding operations out to Great Coates.

THE STAFF OF ARMSTRONG'S WALLPAPER STORES,
at No. 36 Bethlehem Street, taken in 1905.

JOHN BROWNE'S PHOTOGRAPHER'S SHOP and
Septimus Withers' West End Fruit Store in the
late 1870s. The shops occupied Nos 37 and
39 Victoria Street, near the Brewery Street
corner, a site now entirely swallowed up by
Barclays Bank.

JOHN OAKES' CYCLE SHOP at No. 9 East St Mary's Gate, where he moved to in 1898 from round the corner at South St Mary's Gate.

JAMES PLASTOW & SON'S MOTOR-CYCLE SHOP at Nos 13–15 Osborne Street, in the early 1920s, and full of machines with nostalgic names such as Norton and Royal Enfield. The same premises were occupied for a time by Freddy Frith, before he transferred his business to its current premises in Victoria Street.

Above:

FREDERICK LAKE MARRIS' CHEMIST'S SHOP at No. 17 Corporation Road on the corner of Rendel Street. As well as dispensing drugs and patent remedies, Marris was, rather interestingly, licensed to deal in tobacco and cigars. The photograph was taken c. 1905.

Right:

THE INTERIOR of Frederick Marris' shop, c. 1905.

ALBERT D. WALKER, boot and shoe repairer, stands on the left of the photograph outside his shop at No. 68 Pasture Street. The picture was probably taken in the late 1920s.

BYRON V. BAUCKHAM'S 'TRADE-PLATE', with its scrolls and flourishes, and every word in a different face shows him to be a highly competent craftsman. This photograph of his family was taken c. 1906 at their home-workshop at No. 73 Thesiger Street.

THE STAFF AT TICKLER'S FIRST JAM FACTORY in Hope Street, c. 1892. Tickler's jams achieved lasting fame (or notoriety, depending on one's point of view) during the First World War when the preserves – in rather unusual fruit combinations – were supplied to soldiers in the trenches on the Western Front. A well-known Bairnsfather cartoon, in which the humble jam pot was immortalized, suggested that they might not have been universally popular!

THE SORTING-ROOM at the new post office in Victoria Street, taken 5 March 1910. The building was formally opened by the Postmaster-General, the Right Honourable Herbert Samuel MP, just over a month later on 28 April.

POSTMEN outside the new Victoria Street post office, 1910.

THE STAR TEA COMPANY'S SHOP at No. 17 Freeman Street, taken in the early 1890s. Originally a prohibitively expensive seventeenth-century luxury, tea-drinking gradually filtered down the social scale throughout the eighteenth century, and by the end of the nineteenth was one of the national foods. However, even by the the century's end, it was still a commodity that poorer people tended to buy in very small quantities; it was not uncommon for tea to be sold 'by the spoonful'. Presumably the rather startling array of free gifts on offer here represented an effort by the retailer to change the tea-buying habits of generations and encourage their customers to purchase slightly larger quantities.

WORKERS, AND SOME OF THEIR CHILDREN, at Hewitt's Brewery c. 1900. Hewitt Brothers were at one time the largest brewing organization in Lincolnshire. The brewery itself was in Pasture Street (on the site of the present Crown Courts) and there were also maltings, bottling plants and ware-housing in Victoria Street, Burgess Street, Osborne Street and the Bull Ring. The business remained under family control until 1930, when, fol-lowing the death of T.W.G. Hewitt, it became a public company.

THE YOUNG MAN WITH THE LARGE DOG standing at the corner of Garden Street and South St Mary's gate, is one George Capes, whose father owned the grocer's shop of which the building on the corner is a part. The photograph was taken in 1891.

MRS NANCY DAWN'S DINING ROOM at Nos 105 and 107 Cleethorpe Road, strategically located to collect the docks trade at Riby Square. The photograph was taken in the late 1880s.

THE CROSSING-KEEPER'S HOUSE ON WEELSBY ROAD, taken in 1895, when the house stood in open country. The gate-keeper pictured here with his wife is Charles Collins, who inherited the job from his father in the 1860s, and was himself approaching retirement. The construction of the underpass on Weelsby Road in 1933 made the keeper's post, and the cottage, redundant, and the building was demolished in May 1933.

THE STAFF OF THE WEST END LAUNDRY in Cromwell Road, c. 1908. Back row, left to right: H. Thompson (van-driver), -?- , -?- , E. Clark, J. Little, H. Clark. Centre row: Miss Harrison (manageress), -?- , Mrs Bemrose, -?- , -?- , -?- , Jabez Clift (proprietor). Bottom row: A. Wilkinson, N. Blow, F. Little, and Fanny Ann Clift, the other proprietor.

GRIMSBY TELEPHONE EXCHANGE on the corner of Victoria Street and Grime Street in the late 1930s.

THE WORK-FORCE AT GEORGE NICKERSON'S SAWMILLS at Wellowgate, in the 1890s. At the time this photograph was taken, Hickson described himself as 'estate carpenter, wood dealer and maker of gates, sheep hurdles, ladders, tumbrils, sheep troughs, net stakes, thatch pegs, etc ...' By 1922, although the firm was still in business, it was only as a 'manufacturer of poultry houses'.

CASTING UP A FEW SMALL JOBS at Harper Phillips' Albion Foundry in Eastgate, 1933.

EXCAVATING THE SUBWAY under the Great Northern Railway at Weelsby Road in 1933. The narrow level crossing, on one of the main arteries into Grimsby, was a source of constant delays. An early proposal to construct an underpass was a casualty of the First World War and while the scheme was resurrected in 1919, the longed-for work did not begin until May 1933. The bridge, which carried the Louth–Grimsby railway, was built by Dorman, Lang & Co. of Middlesborough.

A SPLENDID STEAM TRACTION-ENGINE belonging to J.C. Clarke's haulage firm, standing in front of C. & C. Wright's, iron and steel merchants, at California siding in Queen Street. The photograph was taken c. 1919/20.

Leisure and Recreation

A GROUP OF COLLECTORS in one of the 'Biggest Ever' hospital parades, c. 1930, standing outside St James' Church.

MR E.R. BENTON'S HIGHLY SUCCESSFUL LADIES' CHOIR, pictured in the 1920s. On the back row is a very youthful Alec Redshaw, who accompanied the choir. He later became the conductor of the Grimsby Philharmonic, and a distinguished adjudicator at Music Festivals in various parts of the country. He is commemorated by Grimsby's International Singing Competition.

ST JAMES' CHURCH CHOIR at Church House in the 1860s. Standing immediately to the right behind the vicar, the Reverend Robert Ainslie, is Anderson Bates, solicitor and local historian and one of the leading figures of the day in Grimsby society.

VICTORIA STREET in 1919. The placard on the unpretentious little Victorian shops announces, in best post-war hyperbole, that the site has been acquired 'for the erection of a magnificent super-cinema and tea rooms . . .' This did indeed become the splendid Savoy Cinema, later the Odeon, and is currently a fast food bar.

THE RIVERHEAD, with the Lyric in the centre of the picture. The Lyric, described as a 'Cinema Theatre', was one of a group of theatres, which included the Prince of Wales in Freeman Street, owned by Grimsby Councillor Joseph Henry Curry.

THE MEN RESPONSIBLE FOR THE MUCH-ADMIRED PEOPLE'S PARK in the 1920s: gardeners from Grimsby Corporation's Parks staff.

FEEDING THE SWANS in People's Park, c. 1905.

A MOTOR BOAT was kept on the lake in People's Park in the 1920s, to run pleasure trips around the central island. The voyage lasted only about five or six minutes, and when the water-level was low, the boat was unable to cross the sewer pipe that runs across to the island, and had to go back the way it had come. Nevertheless, *Florence* was a popular novelty and by the time she was retired, had more than paid for herself. The young man standing on the left in the boat is Arthur Craggs, who joined the gardeners in People's Park as a stable boy just before the First World War.

'SPEAK HANDS FOR ME!' Betogaed citizens of Rome in People's Park wave suitably bloodied daggers over their erstwhile emperor, c. 1880.

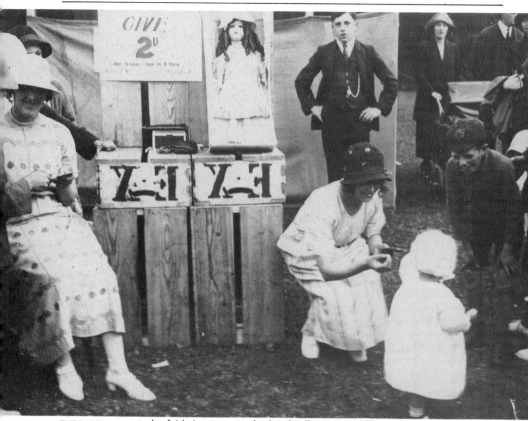

THE BABY seems to be fairly immune to the hard sell approach! The doll was being raffled at the Orphan Home Gala in People's Park, c. 1930. The orphan home was the St Anthony Orphanage, in Victor Street, which had started as a home for boy apprentices, opened by the Grimsby Ice Company in 1891. By 1898, there were insufficient boy apprentices (they being a phenomenon of sail, rather than steam, fishing) and the large building was taken over by the Grimsby, Cleethorpes and East Coast Orphan Home – largely financed by smack-owner Thomas Campbell – who ran it until 1901, when the sisters of the Order of St Joseph of Peace took responsibility for it.

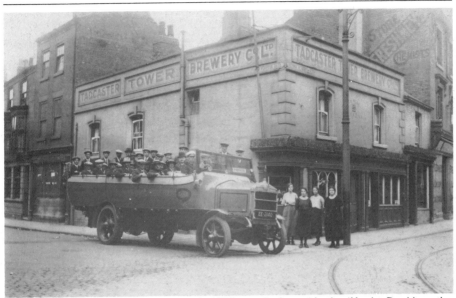

A STAG OUTING BY CHARABANC in the early 1920s, parked outside the 'Mucky Duck', as the Black Swan was familiarly called. This was the oldest public house in Grimsby – there had been an inn on the site from at least the 1650s – but had undergone several metamorphoses by the time this photograph was taken. This version was demolished in 1925, and replaced by another which survived until 1971.

A CHARABANC OUTING outside the Honest Lawyer at Nos 140–2 Kent Street in the 1920s.

THE GEORGE STREET WESLEYAN METHODIST CHAPEL CHOIR, pictured at their picnic outing to Riby Park, c. 1905.

A SALVATION ARMY BAND playing in Garden Street, at the turn of the century. William Booth's 'Army' represented the last great evangelical revival in Britain. Part of its mass appeal lay in his enthusiasm for coloured uniforms and street bands; equally significant was Booth's insistence that social work and care for the material welfare of the poor should be an essential part of the Salvation Army's spiritual mission.

THE ITALIANATE PRINCE OF WALES THEATRE, in about 1901. The theatre was opened in 1884 and less than two years later it was closed for just over four months while it was extensively remodelled to provide, among other things, seating for 2,500 patrons, which made it the largest theatre in Lincolnshire at the time.

THE FINAL PERFORMANCE at the Prince of Wales Theatre before it shut its doors for the very last time.

THE END OF THE PRINCE OF WALES THEATRE. 'Carry's', as it was alternatively known, finally closed its doors in 1936, and the demolition gang moved in. The ABC cinema currently stands on the site.

CHARRED BEAMS BESTREW THE AUDITORIUM in front of the battered proscenium arch of what was the Paragon Cinema in Corporation Road, burned down in 1936.

THE STAFF OF THE HIPPODROME MUSIC HALL in New Market Street, c. 1909. In the centre of the second row, sporting a fine moustache, is the pianist, a Mr Wellings.

THE GAIETY IN WINTRINGHAM ROAD in its previous existence, before the First World War, as a roller-skating rink. Roller-skating has come into and gone out of fashion throughout the twentieth century, and the Gaiety was built for one of the first waves of enthusiasm for the craze. Eventually, as the enthusiasm died and the skating sessions gradually dwindled, the Gaiety became first a much-loved dance-hall and later a discotheque named 'Tiffany's'. Sold again, the premises declined steadily amid repeated complaints from local residents, and was eventually destroyed by fire in 1988.

'PROFESSOR' FREDERICK W. HOFFMAN, one-time manager of the Victoria Music Hall in Lower Burgess Street. His premises had a fairly evil reputation, being among other things, a well-known haunt of prostitutes. In 1883 Hoffman applied for a renewal of his licence for the hall which was turned down following objections from the police. This turned out to be less of a problem for Hoffman than might have been expected, as his (fully-insured) premises were mysteriously burned out a few days later.

THE THEATRE ROYAL IN VICTORIA STREET, known for some obscure reason as the Old Drum, according to Bob Lincoln. Although assuring his readers that the licensee of the theatre engaged 'the best of talent', Lincoln's account of a seriously moral play on the iniquities of drink, performed by a slightly inebriated cast, does make one doubt his truthfulness: 'In one of the scenes, the hero of the piece said to the victim "Whither shall I go?" To our surprise and ... delight, the villain replied "Go to Wigan." Instead ... the hero closed with the said villain ...'

THE BRIGHT SPRING SUNSHINE was clearly causing one or two problems for these little girls, as the May Queen and her attendants at Welholme School, pose for their photograph, c. 1928.

PARTICIPANTS IN THE MAY QUEEN FESTIVITIES organized by the Clee branch of the Labour Party in Weelsby Street, just before the First World War. Margaret Bishop (not pictured) was the May Queen, Selina Randall is third from the left.

MAY DAY at Edward Street School in 1932.

OLD MARKET PLACE with the Statute Fair or 'Stattus' in full swing, c. 1902. Grimsby's right to hold an annual fair dates back to the original Charter of 1201, granted by King John. Grimsby was also one of the last towns in Lincolnshire to hold a hiring, or 'mop' fair, the annual event at which farm and domestic servants were hired for the year.

A RATHER LOWRY-ESQUE PHOTOGRAPH of Grimbarians sliding on the frozen yacht pond, c. 1884.

THIS GROUP OF PRETTY SHOP-GIRLS from James H. Gee's draper's shop in Freeman Street was enjoying the summer sunshine in July 1925.

THE INDOOR RIDING-SCHOOL, known as The Lindens, which was behind the barracks in Augusta Street. The school was run by a Major J.F. Bainbridge of Riby, presumably the very upright gentleman in a bowler hat, mounted on the far left of the photograph, seen with a group of his pupils.

THE LIONS AT BEECHFIELD ZOO, which was at the end of College Street, taken c. 1930.

THE WORSLEY CRICKET CLUB was probably the leading club in Grimsby in the 1860s, when this photograph was taken. The club's field lay at the, then, end of Willingham Street, just past the crossroads with Catherine Street. Despite a successful sporting record – a number of its members played in the Grimsby & District team against the United South of 1876, in which W.G. Grace was 400 not out – the club was in chronic financial difficulties for most of its life, and in 1894 it was wound up and the ground sold.

FLOTTERGATE CHURCH (i.e. the Methodist Chapel) cricket team, 1906.

GRIMSBY VICTORIA CRICKET TEAM. In the pavilion, from left to right: A. Ousey, W. Brocklesby, J. Ellis jun., J. Ellis sen. Below: J. Earle, G. Golding, A. Burnham, W. Taylor, H. Evans, Bob Lincoln and T. Atkinson.

THE 'OLD WINGHAMS' CRICKET CLUB TEAM PHOTOGRAPH, taken on the very eve of the Second World War. Back row, from left to right: G. Gifford, H. Green, E. Wilson (Chairman), L. Bennett, A. Walsham, B. Bennett. Front row: H. Vincent, N. Bennett, N. Heath (Vice Capt.), J. Stapley (Captain), R. Jackson, R. Johnson, R. Normandale. All were ex-pupils of Wintringham School.

GRIMSBY ALL SAINTS FOOTBALL CLUB were the leading amateur side in the town at the end of the nineteenth century, and were regarded as something of a nursery for the professional Grimsby Town. Some, at least, of these boys in the club's junior side could hope for the chance of a more-or-less glittering sporting career.

THE FIRST GRIMSBY TOWN FOOTBALL TEAM, 1879. Back row, from left to right: A.M. Read, R.C. Hall, Bob Lincoln, F. Marshall, J. Warner, A. Ousey, W.T. Lammin. Front row: S. Noble, H. Monument, J. France, T. Atkinson, F. Lowe.

GRIMSBY TOWN FOOTBALL CLUB'S FINANCES were often in a parlous state, but in the very severe winter of 1898/9, when matches had to be postponed, reserves reached an all-time low. Mr W.H. Bellamy organized an archery tournament to raise funds, with prizes provided by friends of the club. Unfortunately, for various reasons, the contest was postponed, and when it was eventually held, raised only £29 for the club. The committee were, from left to right: Back row: ? Needler, J.B. Bellamy, J.W. Taylor, C. White, W.H. Bellamy, A. Flint, W. Rogerson. Front row: H.N. Hickson, A. Martin, W.J.P. Whitsed, T.J. Bradley, A. Burnham, J. Plastow.

A CYCLISTS' MEET OUTSIDE GRIMSBY TOWN HALL in 1885, with some remarkable contraptions sporting two, three and four wheels. The gentleman in the centre of the photograph perched on his 'ordinary' with a bugle round his neck was the cycling club's captain. The bugle was used to communicate directions to the other club members when they cycled *en masse*.

Bottom, left:
WELHOLME SCHOOL FOOTBALL CLUB, with the Atkinson Cup and the League Shield, which was presented to the Grimsby & District Schools Sport Association by the *Grimsby Times and Telegraph* for elementary schools in Grimsby and Cleethorpes. The 1920/1 side were, from left to right. Back row: Mr Langley, Mr Barker, Mr Horn. Centre row: Mr Turner, Bill Newmarsh, Frank Bee, George Anfield, Harry Shadlow, Johnny Dawson, Bunty Collins, Cyril Bough. Front row: Lew Sempers, Ken Robinson, Jack Rutter and Reg Miller.

'POPULAR JIMMY', James Plastow, a fish salesman and leading light of Grimsby Cyclists' Club, standing outside his home at No. 43 Orwell Street with his 'ordinary' and an impressive array of trophies, prizes and medals won by him with it during the 1880s.

GRIMSBY CYCLISTS' CLUB, taken in the 1880s at their premises in No. 22 South St Mary's Gate. In the foreground is an ordinary or penny farthing, the machine which, in bicycle evolution, comes after the iron-tyred velocipede – the craze of the 1860s – and before the safety bicycle of the 1890s, the 'working-man's friend', which brought cycling to the masses. The ordinary was an enthusiasm for the relatively well-heeled. When this photograph was taken they would have cost between £12 and £25, effectively beyond the scope of the ordinary artisan. The later safety bicylces, on the other hand, could be bought new for £4.50, and there was a flourishing second-hand trade.

Bottom, left:
THE START for the National Cyclists' Union 25-mile Championship, 'open to the world', held on the Worsley Cinder track in 1888. This was the first year that the national organization had allotted a championship race to the Grimsby track. There were ten entrants, only one of whom, R.M. Wright, came from Grimsby. The race was eventually won in great style by J.H. Adams of Speedwell Bicycle Club, with H. Synyer of Nottingham second and F.B. Woods of Brixton third. The photograph was taken by William Garthwaite.

CHARLES HORN, MASTER BAKER, of Heneage Road, taking his family for a spin in 1909.

ALL READY FOR THE GRIMSBY HOSPITAL PARADE in the 1920s.

MARK NEAL, who ran a confectionary business at No. 320 Victoria Street, with his mother and children in their trap at Nun's corner, c. 1905.

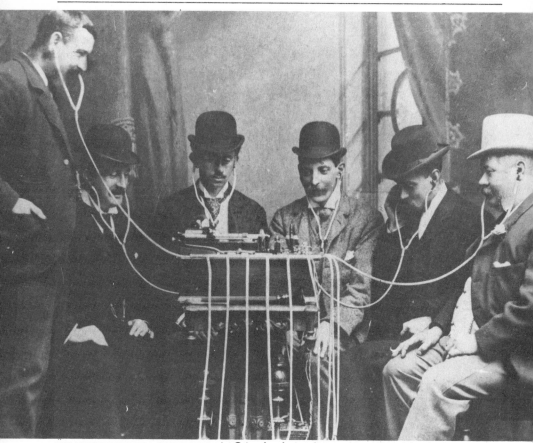

THE FIRST ELECTRICAL PHONOGRAPH in Grimsby, being listened to with evident enjoyment by, among others, 'Professor' Dent of the Hippodrome (third from left), and H.J. Curry, owner of the Prince of Wales Theatre. The phonograph was invented by the American Thomas Edison (and tested by its inventor with the words of 'Mary had a little lamb'!) but did not really begin to come into its own until the 1890s. This photograph was taken c. 1895.

ROAD ROLLER-SKATING TO HEALING, one of the events organized in June 1930 for the support of the Grimsby and District Hospital.

SMALL BOYS FISHING enthusiastically (if not altogether successfully, judging by the jam jars) at the Riverhead in 1937.

GRIMSBY BOWLING CLUB at their ground in Brighowgate in 1896. Top row, from left to right: H. Bolton, J. Emptage, R. Northcote, Sam Haddlesey, A. Cook, H. Cook, William Skelton, Bob Lincoln, A. Longridge, A. Robinson & M. Cook. Centre, seated: J. Cook, F. Mason, J. Broadhead, R. Johnson, R. Mason and David Smith. Front, seated: and C.S. Hall, Alfred Wykes, A. Skelton and J. Taylor.

SECTION FIVE

Events

CARNIVAL TIME in the 1920s.

THE RELIEF OF MAFEKING in May 1900, after a protracted siege by the Boers, aroused a fury of patriotic fervour. On Saturday 19 May, a carnival procession was held (seen here rounding Palmer's Corner into Victoria Street), a special broadsheet souvenir, the *Mafeking Reliever*, was published, and the celebrations were rounded off by a torchlight procession from Riby Square and a late-night cinematographic performance of military pictures outside the cycling club premises in Hainton Square.

THE SECOND DAY OF FESTIVITIES to celebrate the Coronation of King George V in June 1911 was taken over with a procession of children to People's Park, where they were to be presented with souvenir medals by the Mayor, Councillor Whitely Wilkin, and given tea by Sir George and Lady Doughty. The event was marred by the weather; the children (16,992 of them, and their teachers) are seen here walking down Doughty Road in the sunshine, but long before they reached the park, the heavens opened and the marchers were well and truly drenched.

Bottom, left:
A CYCLIST PEDALS CAREFULLY ACROSS THE TRAM TRACKS at Hainton Square, in June 1902. Freeman Street is alive with flags and bunting in celebration of Edward VII's coronation.

AN EARLY DUTY FOR GEORGE V was the opening, on 22 July 1912, of the new docks at Immingham. The royal couple arrived by train and were driven down Victoria Street in brilliant sunshine to the Dock station. At Lock Hill, shown here, a stand was filled with local schoolchildren, who serenaded the king and queen with a lusty rendition of 'What can I do for England?' followed by a verse of the National Anthem.

HOPE STREET, always famous for the enormous effort that the residents put into their street decorations, is seen here living up to its reputation in celebration of the Queen Elizabeth II's coronation in June 1953.

THE ANCIENT ORDER OF DRUIDS FRIENDLY SOCIETY parading at Hainton Square at the 1909 Biennial General Assembly.

THE PRINCE OF WALES (later, briefly Edward VIII) being driven along Hainton Avenue. The Prince visited Grimsby on 19 July 1928, to open the new Corporation Bridge.

DURING THE COURSE OF HIS VISIT TO GRIMSBY, the Prince of Wales was taken to the docks. He is seen here (second on the gang-plank, in the black bowler) boarding the steam trawler *Rolls Royce*.

CROWDS MASSED IN CENTRAL MARKET in an effort to catch a glimpse of the Prince of Wales arriving to open Corporation Bridge.

THE CHIEF SCOUT, LIEUTENANT-GENERAL SIR ROBERT BADEN-POWELL, founder of the Scout movement and hero of the Boer War, visited Grimsby on 22 May 1911 as part of a week of inspections in north Lincolnshire. He is seen here (second from left, talking to a scout) in People's Park, his inspection well under way.

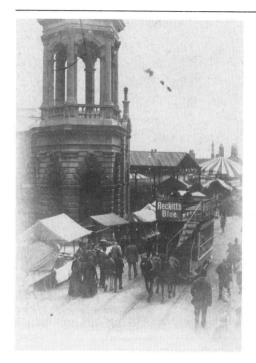

THE CORN EXCHANGE, with the gaily-striped tent in the background, indicating that it was not only a market day, but the stattus fair was also in town. Judging by the bustles on the women's dresses, the photograph was taken in the mid-1880s. Horse trams finally ceased to be used in Grimsby in 1901.

A MOCK-UP OF LINCOLN'S STONEBOW at Holme Hill, to celebrate the 1904 Lincolnshire Show held at Grimsby.

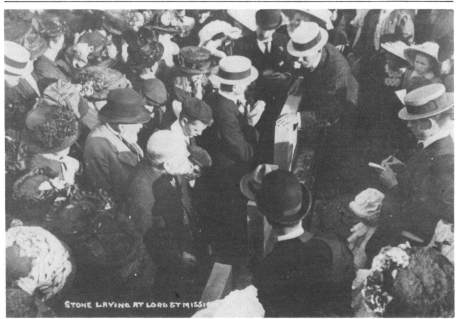

STONE-LAYING at the Primitive Methodist Lord Street Mission Hall.

THE 'WILKINSON' 1935 TL MERRYWEATHER FIRE ENGINE and crew outside Queen Mary's hostel in Riby Square in 1938, collecting for the 'Boots for the Bairns' fund. The crew, from left to right, are: A. Bowles, S. Mackay (on the engine), R. Pike, H. Sargent, G. Woods, P. Parkinson (on the engine), Stan Smith and J. Robinson.

GRIMSBY BOROUGH FIREMEN proudly displaying their new equipment in People's Park, c. 1906. At this time, the Corporation Fire Brigade possessed two steam fire engines, the water in the boilers of which being kept 'constantly hot by gas jets', and with fires very reassuringly 'laid ready for lighting at a moment's notice'. Their newest acquisition was rather more fully described as a 'Combination Motor Hose Carriage, Fire Escape and Chemical Engine, capacity 40 gallons, and 35 horse power'.

Bottom, right:

THE LIFEBOAT SATURDAY PROCESSION passing along Freeman Street on 22 August 1903. The B.W. Smith on the centre wagon was Brader William Smith, a large timber merchant. The Royal National Lifeboat Institution at this time had a boat house in the Fish Dock basin, replacing the original local lifeboat station at Cleethorpes in 1882. In 1887, this vessel was replaced by the *Charles Burton*, which remained in Grimsby until 1927, when it was decided that the entire Humber Estuary could be covered by the motor lifeboat at Spurn.

A MOTLEY COLLECTION OF CYCLISTS joining in the fun of the 1930 Hospital Carnival.

ONE OF THE MORE SPECTACULAR WEDDINGS of the 1920s. Mr Haith, the groom, was a keeper at Grimsby's Beechfield Zoo. His bride appears less than amused to find that she had to walk from her wedding with Rosie the elephant in tow.

THE CIRCUS COMES TO TOWN. An unusual cargo arrives by rail, courtesy of Bertram Mills circus in October 1955. The cooling towers from the Doughty Road power-station can be seen in the background.

DECLARING THE POLL AT GRIMSBY 1906

THE GENERAL ELECTION of 1906 was a three-cornered fight between Sir George Doughty, H.H. Haldinstein, the Liberal candidate and, for the first time in Grimsby, a Labour Party candidate, Tom Proctor.

THE RT HON LLOYD GEORGE M.P.
TOM WING ESQ M.P.

TOM WING'S CANDIDATURE in the January 1911 General Election was the result of an amicable arrangement between the Liberals and the infant Labour Party. The Liberal Government was apparently most anxious to unseat the sitting Conservative member, Sir George Doughty. Lloyd George himself appeared and spoke at the Wintringham Road Skating Rink – a visit which may have tipped the balance in a close contest, which gave Wing a majority of 322.

BEADED FLAPPER DRESSES ABOUND at this late 1920s dance, given for the staff of the Coal, Salt and Tanning Co.

THIS SAD LITTLE PHOTOGRAPH is a reminder of what was once an all-too-common sight in Victorian and Edwardian times. Taken in August 1901, at the corner of Brewery Street and Victoria Street, it shows the pathetic aftermath of an eviction, with the contents of the building heaped unceremoniously out on the pavement.

THE FUNERAL PROCESSION for the victims of the HMS *Cobra* disaster, winding through the Old Market Place, 23 September 1901. The torpedo boat destroyer was lost off Spurn when she struck the Gudgeon Rocks on her way to Portsmouth from her Newcastle builders to be commissioned. Six of the sixty lost were landed at Grimsby.

MOURNERS AND ONLOOKERS at the funeral of William Grange who died shortly before his ninety-second birthday on 12 June 1913. The funeral service was held at the George Street Wesleyan chapel, and afterwards the entire Corporation, headed by the Mayor, Christopher Miller, processed to Scartho Road Cemetery.

People and Personalities

A STUDIO PORTRAIT by H. Jancowski of the Greenfield family, c. 1898.

GRIMSBY BOROUGH POLICE, 1878, outside the Town Hall. The police force in the mid-1860s were not altogether the fine upstanding body of law-keepers that this photograph might suggest. In 1858 the entire force was dismissed after complaints of misconduct. The new force did their job, after a fashion, but there were repeated tales in the press about constables emerging from brothels, blackmailing publicans, fighting each other while on duty, forgetting to lock their prisoners up and, most frequently of all, being discovered drunk. However, they must have made a certain impact; by 1878, it was generally said that most of the underworld had moved to New Clee, then outside the Borough boundary.

JOHN STIRLING, Chief Constable of Grimsby from 1901 to 1931, in full dress uniform.

A POLICE SERGEANT with a female burglar, photographed in the 1860s.

SERGEANT SAUNBY of the Grimsby Borough Police, c. 1905.

JOHN STIRLING (with arms folded) pictured shortly before his retirement as Chief Constable of the Grimsby Borough Police Force, with former members of his force who had themselves subsequently become chief constables elsewhere.

ZACRY WILKINSON WOODS (1873–1935), Superintendent of the Grimsby Borough Fire Brigade, with 'Mick', taken c. 1920–5.

GRIMSBY BOROUGH FIRE BRIGADE, taken at Cleethorpes in 1890.

TWO MEMBERS OF THE FORMER GRIMSBY BOROUGH FIRE BRIGADE. Above, Sergeant S.J. Mackay, photographed by Edwin Noble and, below, Jack Oakes, photographed by Stanley J. Warren in the 1930s.

THOMAS BRIGG'S TOBACCONIST'S SHOP and the Railway Tavern on Cleethorpe Road, at the junction with Railway Street, taken c. 1880. While Mr Briggs and his shop have long since vanished into the mists of time, the pub achieved a kind of immortality as the birthplace of Dame Madge Kendal, the celebrated actress, whose itinerant thespian parents were temporarily lodging there. Among the many honours heaped on her in later life, Dame Madge was granted the Freedom of Grimsby, and a ward at the Scartho Road Hospital was named after her.

THE EIGHTY-YEAR-OLD DAME MADGE KENDAL (Madge Robertson) at Grimsby Hospital on 14 October 1928.

THE GRAND OLD MAN OF GRIMSBY, WILLIAM GRANGE, probably taken on his ninety-first birthday on 10 July 1912, when he was fêted as 'The Oldest Town Clerk in England' after fifty-one years in the post. Born in 1821 and educated at the Freeman's Grammar School, he succeeded his partner George Babb as town clerk in 1861. A staunch Methodist, his response to the inevitable journalist's question on the occasion of his birthday was 'I am a total abstainer of over forty years standing, and I do not think I have ever smoked a whole cigar.'

MISS MOODY (RIGHT) AND HER CHARGES at Welholme Infants School in 1900. The small boy, dressed entirely in white with his teacher's hand resting protectively on his shoulder, is Roy Freshney.

CLASS THREE AT WELHOLME JUNIOR SCHOOL, c. 1900. The school, at Welholme Road East, was built in 1892 in what was a fast-growing suburb of Grimsby, being developed from the 1870s on the Heneage Estate.

MR WYLD (SEATED) WITH HIS FAMILY in 1892. Mr Wyld was the headmaster of the Garibaldi Primitive Methodist Day School, the only day school run by the Primitives in Grimsby.

WELLOW COTTAGE, in what became Ainslie Street. The gentleman resting outside his barn is probably Jarvis Watson, a cow keeper. The division between town and country in Victorian England was far less clear cut than it is today, and it was not at all unusual to find livestock kept less than a quarter of a mile from the fashionable shopping area.

GYPSIES WITH THEIR CARAVANS outside the Corn Exchange c. 1900.

'TWO-STICK CHARLIE', a well-known Grimsby character in the 1920s and '30s, and famous for his impersonations of Napoleon and Charlie Chaplin.

THIS EXQUISITELY TURNED-OUT VEHICLE, pictured here with its chauffeur outside People's Park, belonged to Alfred J. Knott (his monogram is on the door), one of the three fish-merchant Knott Brothers, who lived at Temple Rhydding, No. 37 Welholme Road.

THE MYSTERIOUS ORIENT COMES TO KENT STREET. Or, to be more precise, the Tower Cinema, where these rather self-conscious usherettes were persuaded to dress up as houris to publicize the opening of a long since forgotten 1920s epic, *The Queen of Sheba*.

MR JOHN JAMES SEARS (left) and his apprentice at B.W. Smith's house furnishers in Freeman Street, c. 1920. Mr Sears was a journeyman french polisher, and he is seen here repolishing organs and pianos, at Smith's workshops in Eleanor Street.

THE CLERICAL STAFF IN THE FISH DEPARTMENT, Great Central Railway Company, employed at Grimsby Docks. The photograph was taken on 8 January 1902.

THIS STUDIO PORTRAIT, unfortunately unidentified, was taken by Lowthian Brothers of Nos 144–6 Freeman Street. The subject was a trooper of the Imperial Yeomanry, many regiments of which were raised specifically for service in the Boer War of 1899–1902. He may well have been a member of the Lincolnshire Imperial Yeomanry, which was raised in 1901 and which never actually saw service in South Africa, but the uniform, alas, has nothing which specifically identifies it as belonging to any particular regiment.

SECTION SEVEN

Grimsby at War

YOUTHFUL GRIMBARIANS at an Officer Training Corps Camp, July 1914.

MEN WHO ENLISTED INTO THE VOLUNTEER ARMY of 1914/15 were formed into local companies and battalions of the county regiment, the philosophy being that men would fight better together, if they knew each other to begin with. The 10th Battalion of the Lincolnshire Regiment was familiarly known as the 'Grimsby Chums', and in a relatively small town like Grimsby, if the men did not actually know each other personally, most would have friends or acquaintances in common. The grim drawback of this policy was brought home to Grimsby on 1 July 1916, when the 1,000-strong battalion was put in the front line on the first day of the Battle of the Somme. By the end of the day, just over half of them had been killed, wounded or were 'missing'. Losses on this scale, with the devastating effect that they had on the home community, caused a revision of official thinking, and recruitment into 'Chums' battalions was discontinued.

GRIMSBY & CLEETHORPES VOLUNTEER TRAINING CORPS ready for inspection at People's Park, 15 March 1915. The man standing in front of them is Charlie Wilmott.

THE CHUMS DID THEIR BASIC TRAINING IN BROCKLESBY PARK and, in May 1915, left the area for advanced training. Before they left, the battalion staged a farewell march from Cleethorpes Railway station via Freeman Street to People's Park, where they were officially welcomed by the Mayor, Councillor J.W. Eason. From the park they then marched to Grimsby Town station, following a rather circuitous route through Dudley Street, Littlefield Lane, Corporation Road and Victoria Street. They are seen here in Hainton Avenue.

FLIGHT LIEUTENANT EDWARD GORDON RIGGAL RN, 1895–1915. Edward Riggall was born in Grimsby and educated at Humberstone's Foundation School where he was school captain. He was killed in action at Ostend, on 16 February 1915, barely six months into the First World War.

GEORGE V AND QUEEN MARY at Grimsby docks greeting war-workers, April 1918.

DURING THE FIRST WORLD WAR, Weelsby Hall, the home of the Sleight family, was offered for use as a convalescent home for soldiers wounded on the Western Front. Sergeant Charles Williams of Louth is on the extreme right of this quartet, taken in 1916.

THIS PICTURE IS NOT *ENTIRELY* WHAT IT SEEMS. The 'pretty maids' are in fact, like the other members of the party, Grimsby fishermen, who were unlucky enough to be in German ports or territorial waters when war was declared with Britain in August 1914. They were interned at Ruhleben, a converted trotting stadium on the outskirts of Berlin, and enlivened their incarceration by evolving a highly-organized programme of entertainments, lectures, classes, services, and the production of a very professional camp magazine. This picture, taken in 1916, was of the cast of one of the many dramatic productions.

FILLING SANDBAGS during the summer of 1939, at the corner of the Doughty Road–Ainslie Street recreation ground.

THE NEWLY-CONSTRUCTED MUNICIPAL OFFICES, shrouded in camouflage netting to protect the building from aerial attack, c. 1943.

AN ARP TENDER AND CREW, C. 1942.

A GRIMSBY HOME GUARD UNIT relaxing at training camp during the Second World War.

THE AUXILIARY FIRE SERVICE (Wellow Section) with appliances outside the Lincolnshire Motor Company's premises at No. 39 Wellowgate, c. 1939.

DEALING WITH AN UNEXPLODED BOMB sunk deep into the clay of a Grimsby garden, c. 1942.

MADDISON'S CORNER, the junction of Victoria Street and Pasture Street, taken early one May evening in 1942. The glass door of the baker's shop is protected by a cross of the ubiquitous brown sticky tape to cut down the danger of injury from flying glass in the event of a bomb blast.

OLD MARKET PLACE during the Second World War. The 'S' poster outside the Corn Exchange marks the entrance to one of the communal air raid shelters.

A WARTIME AMBULANCE parked in Park Drive, c. 1939. The white paint on the mudguards was to assist in the black-out.

CENTRAL MARKET, with servicemen outside Victoria House, 1942.

ONE OF THE MANY STREET PARTIES held in Grimsby to celebrate VE Day. This one was in First Avenue, on the Nunsthorpe estate.

ACKNOWLEDGEMENTS

I am most grateful to Mr F.H. Hills, Assistant Director of Leisure & Economic Development, Great Grimsby Borough Council, for the permission to use the photographs from the Welholme Galleries collection. In addition to those from the Hallgarth Collection, the following people have made their photographs available:

Mrs Baker • Mr D. Barley • Mrs M. Bennett • Mr F. Brewster • Mrs Borrill
Mr J. Brown • Mrs R. Burton • Mrs Calder • Mr D. Campbell
Mr P. Chessman • Mrs J. Chevins • Mr Coates • Mr D.A. Cole • Consolidated
Fisheries Ltd • Mr S. Cormack • Mr A. Craggs • Mr F. Davies • Mrs H. Dean
Mr J. Elliott • Mrs Featherstone • Mrs Fitton • Mr G.H. Fowler
Miss Freshney • Mrs Goldberg • Mr Ingram • Mr C.W. Lawson • Mr A.V. Lond
Mr G. Mackay • Mr J.C. Mawer • Mr Mercer • Mr Miller • Mr Norton
Mrs Pyke • Mr Roberts • Mr Sharkey • Mr R. Simons • Mr A. Smith
Mrs J. Smith • Wm. Stones (Brewers) Ltd • Mr Storey • Mrs Templeman
Mrs Tierney • Mr B. Tomlinson • Mrs M. Vincent • Mr Wakelin
Mr G.A.Watkinson • Mrs West • Mrs J. Wivell • Mr L. Woods.

I should also like to thank Mrs Lola Grosset for her skilled decoding of my hieroglyphics and converting them to legible typescript.